EASTER | Recipes, Gifts & Decorations

EASTER | Recipes, Gifts & Decorations

Beautiful ideas for springtime festivities, with 30 delightful flower
displays, traditional recipes, crafted eggs and decorative gifts,
including over 130 evocative and inspirational photographs

Tessa Evelegh

southwater

This edition is published by Southwater

Southwater is an imprint of Anness Publishing Limited
Hermes House 88–89 Blackfriars Road London SE1 8HA
tel. 020 7401 2077; fax 020 7633 9499;
www.southwaterbooks.com; www.annesspublishing.com

If you like the images in this book and would like to investigate using
them for publishing, promotions or advertising, please visit our website
www.practicalpublishing.com for more information.

UK agent: The Manning Partnership Ltd;
tel. 01225 478444; fax 01225 478440; sales@manning-partnership.co.uk
UK distributor: Grantham Book Services Ltd;
tel. 01476 541080; fax 01476 541061; orders@gbs.tbs-ltd.co.uk
North American agent/distributor: National Book Network;
tel. 301 459 3366; fax 301 429 5746; www.nbnbooks.com
Australian agent/distributor: Pan Macmillan Australia; tel. 1300 135 113;
fax 1300 135 103; customer.service@macmillan.com.au
New Zealand agent/distributor: David Bateman Ltd;
tel. (09) 415 7664; fax (09) 415 8892

A CIP catalogue record for this book is available from the British Library.

Publisher: Joanna Lorenz
Project Editor: Sarah Ainley
Editorial Reader: Hayley Kerr
Copy Editor: Beverley Jollands
Designer: Lilian Lindblom
Illustrations: Anna Koska

ETHICAL TRADING POLICY
Because of our ongoing ecological investment programme, you, as our
customer, can have the pleasure and reassurance of knowing that a tree is
being cultivated on your behalf to naturally replace the materials used to
make the book you are holding. For further information about this
scheme, go to www.annesspublishing.com/trees

Previously published as *Easter: A Celebration*

ACKNOWLEDGEMENTS
The publishers would like to thank the following for contributing projects to this book:
Fiona Barnett pp10–11, 18–19, 20–1, 28–9, 36; Jacqueline Clark and Joanna Farrow pp58; Stephanie Donaldson pp40–1, 56;
Tessa Evelegh pp12, 13, 14, 15, 16–17, 22–3, 26–7, 30, 31, 32–3, 36–7, 43, 44–5, 46–7; Gilly Love pp59, 62–3; Janice Murfitt and Louise Pickford pp56–7, 61;
Deborah Schneebeli-Morrell pp38–9, 42, 46, 48–9; Elizabeth Wolf-Cohen pp52–3.
Photography by David Armstrong, Michelle Garrett, Debbie Patterson, Heini Schneebeli and Polly Wreford.

Contents

~

Introduction
~

The enduring symbols of the Easter festival are those of nature itself: the bursting buds of new leaves, the energetic growth of spring flowers, the egg with its potential for new life. The Saxon festival of Eostre, the goddess of dawn, was celebrated annually as winter gave way to spring, and this ancient festival of rebirth was absorbed by the Christian church as its theme corresponded suitably with the resurrection of Christ.

Easter eggs and the Easter rabbit are both pre-Christian symbols of fertility, which have survived into the festival we celebrate today. The egg is a particularly enduring symbol, and nearly every culture has devised styles of ornamenting the shell, or copying the shape in porcelain and precious metals, sugar, marzipan and, of course, chocolate.

At Easter the natural world is bursting with freshness and vitality, and its riches can be garnered to make gifts and decorations of great charm and significance. It is a season of joy and optimism, and a splendid opportunity to celebrate with innovative and traditional treats.

Spring Flowers

~

The year's earliest flowers epitomize nature's annual renewal that is in turn symbolized by the Easter festival. Day by day, green shoots grow almost visibly as if the earth is unable to contain the energy of the new season. The delicate, waxy petals and pure, fresh colours of crocuses, daffodils and tulips belie their strength, as they withstand the showers, gales, frosts and other rigours of unpredictable spring weather. Ethereal blossoms spring from bare branches, raising the spirits after the gloom of winter and full of the promise of a bountiful harvest later in the year.

Tulip pomander

*I*n Elizabethan times pomanders were filled with herbs or scented flowers and carried to perfume the air. Instead of exotic aromas, the sweet scent of newly picked Easter tulips pervades this pomander. Hung from smooth satin ribbon, this charming decoration can be hung indoors or out.

MATERIALS
~
13cm/5in diameter florist's foam ball

2m/2yd satin ribbon

scissors

20 heads 'Appleblossom' double tulips

myrtle stems

stub (floral) wires

wire cutters

reindeer moss

1 Soak the foam ball in water. Tie the ribbon around the ball, starting at the top and crossing it over at the bottom, then tying at the top to divide the ball into four equal segments.

2 Cut the tulip stems to 2.5cm/1in and push them carefully into the foam. Arrange five tulips in a vertical line down the centre of each segment.

3 Cut sprigs of myrtle on short stems and push them into the foam ball to create lines on either side of each line of tulips. The myrtle should appear quite compact.

4 Form short "staples" from sections of stub (floral) wire and use them to pin the reindeer moss to cover any remaining exposed areas of the foam ball.

Simple blossom

*T*he appeal of spring flowers and blossoms lies in their simplicity, and the most pleasing way to display them is to fuss with the flowers as little as possible. Aim to find a complementary container, cut the stems to a length that flatters both flowers and container, and enjoy their natural charm.

Above: Pure white perfumed lilac teamed with fuller white pear blossom makes a most thoughtful bouquet for a guest's bedroom. Tied with an old-gold ribbon and set in a golden glass, it would decorate a dressing table or bedside table delightfully, while exuding its glorious scent.

Left: Snake's-head fritillary must be one of the most pleasing yet unfamiliar spring flowers. Their charming nodding heads, distinctively patterned with checks, and deep green grass-like leaves, are a joy to behold both outdoors and in. They look wonderful in verdigris containers, with their stems left long so the flower heads can dance in a crowd, much as they would in the wild. Add a bowlful of eggs to the display for a really seasonal look.

Spring posies

*T*he word posy originates from the sixteenth-century "poesy", another word for poem or motto, because when floral posies were given, seasonal flowers came wrapped in paper inscribed with a message. These pretty posies evoke the spirit of Easter, and are examples of "messages" that might have been sent in Elizabethan times.

Above: The sharp green alchemilla leaves setting off this posy hold no particular meaning in the language of flowers, but the auriculas indicate beauty.

Right: As an echo of springtime optimism, intense blue hyacinths and the more subtle grape hyacinths are set off beautifully by the vibrant emerald leaves of the latter.

Hearts and flowers

The lushness of ornamental cherry blossom needs no decoration, but in a glass container its woody stems look charming tied and decorated with a raffia heart. Hang more hearts in the branches to complement the display.

1 Cut a length of wire about 30cm/ 12in long, make a hook in each end and link the hooks together. Make a dip in the middle of the wire for the top of the heart.

2 Starting at the dip and leaving a tail free for tying up at the end, begin to bind the wire with the raffia.

3 Bind the raffia densely all around the heart, pulling it taut as you go. Ensure that the wire is completely covered.

4 When you get back to the top, tie the ends together firmly, then make a bow. Cut the cherry blossom branches to a length suitable for the container. Tie them into a bunch using raffia, then tie on the heart and place the arrangement in the vase.

Daffodil and box display

An arrangement of plants in pots looks just as lovely indoors as outside. Here, cheerful nodding narcissi are offset by young, emerald green box plants. In early summer the box can be planted in the garden.

MATERIALS

~

watering can

8 young box plants

5 narcissi bulbs, in bud

8 small terracotta pots

compost (soil mix)

1 large terracotta pot

sphagnum moss

1 Water the plants well and allow them to drain for at least an hour.

2 Re-pot the young box plants in the small terracotta pots, firming in extra compost (soil mix) if needed.

3 Re-pot the bulbs all together in the large terracotta pot, firming in extra compost if needed.

4 Dress the tops of the pots with moss, then arrange the small pots around the large one. Water well, and water again whenever the surface feels dry.

Springtime garland

Garlands of fresh flowers make delightful decorations for an Easter celebration. This pretty little arrangement of pansies and violas has a delicate, woodland feel, and the plants are readily available at this time of year in a range of fresh spring colours.

MATERIALS
~

secateurs (pruners)

chicken-wire, cut to desired length and three times width of garland

scissors

plastic bin liner (trash bag)

2 pansy plants for each 15cm/6in of garland

6 viola plants for each 15cm/6in of garland

stub (floral) wires

moss

1 Using secateurs (pruners), cut the chicken-wire to size and then form it into a flattened roll.

2 Cut the bin liner (trash bag) into squares large enough to wrap the roots of the pansies and violas.

3 One by one, unpot each plant, gently remove any loose soil and place the roots in the centre of a square of bin liner.

4 Gather the plastic around the roots and fix it in place by winding a stub (floral) wire around the top, leaving a short length free to attach to the garland.

5 Secure the bagged-up plants to the garland by twisting round the free ends of the wires.

6 Finish by covering any visible plastic with moss, securing it with short lengths of wire bent into U-shaped "staples".

Scented arrangement

The flowers used for this Easter display are chosen for their distinctive and delicious scents, combining to produce a heady perfume ideal in a hallway or living room. Cream and yellow flowers and foliage create the backdrop for beautiful yellow freesias and powdery mimosa.

MATERIALS

~

florist's foam block

wooden trug

cellophane (plastic wrap)

scissors

20 stems golden privet

10 stems tuberoses

10 stems cream stocks

20 stems freesias

20 stems mimosa

1 Soak the florist's foam and wedge it firmly into the trug, having first lined it with cellophane (plastic wrap). Trim the edges of the cellophane to neaten.

2 Strip the lower leaves from the stems of privet and insert them into the foam to build the outline of the arrangement.

3 Reinforce the outline of the display with the tuberoses and stocks, arranging them in opposing diagonals.

4 Distribute the freesias and mimosa, using a mixture of stem sizes to pull the display together visually.

Easter garland

Easter is a time of hope and regeneration, and this bright wreath visually captures these feelings. The vibrant colours and the flowers, arranged to look as though they are still growing, give the garland a fresh, natural glow. Eggs are included as a symbol of birth, and are attached to the garland with a length of natural raffia.

MATERIALS
~

30cm/12in diameter florist's foam ring

elaeagnus foliage

scissors

5 polyanthus plants

8 pieces bark

stub (floral) wires

70 stems daffodils

natural raffia

3 blown eggs

1 Soak the foam ring in water and arrange an even covering of elaeagnus stems, about 7.5cm/3in long, in the foam. Add groups of three polyanthus leaves at five equidistant positions.

2 Wire each piece of bark by bending a stub (floral) wire around the middle and twisting to achieve a tight grip. Position the pieces of bark evenly around the ring using the wires.

3 Arrange the polyanthus flowers in groups of single colours, leaving a gap for the eggs. Cut the daffodils to a stem length of about 7.5cm/3in and arrange them between the polyanthus, pushing their stems into the foam.

4 Wrap raffia around the blown eggs, crossing it over underneath and tying it on the side. Gently wire the eggs in place in the gap between the flowers. Arrange the remaining polyanthus flowers and daffodils around the eggs.

Springtime wreath

A *few sprigs of fruit blossom and pussy willow can be transformed into a lush seasonal wreath when teamed with the fresh new growth that brings added vigour to evergreens. The foliage here is rosemary, a profuse shrub that benefits from being cut back. Its fragrance awakens the senses and adds to the charm of the wreath.*

MATERIALS
~

20cm/8in diameter florist's foam ring
large bunch of young rosemary shoots
secateurs (pruners)
pussy willow
pear blossom

1 Thoroughly soak the florist's foam ring in water, then snip the rosemary into pieces about 15cm/6in long. Leave some a little longer to give a feathery look to the finished wreath.

2 Push the rosemary into the foam ring, arranging it at an angle so it flows around the circle in one direction. Add the pussy willow, placing most of it at the top of the inside edge for impact.

3 Place most of the pear blossom so that it covers the inside edge of the ring. Add a few blossoms to the outside. Fill any gaps with spare rosemary.

Natural Displays

~

As the days continue to lengthen around Easter, crisp bright mornings filled with sunshine and birdsong entice us outside into the garden and the countryside to sense for ourselves the resurgence of the natural world. Like the birds busily collecting materials to complete their new nests, we instinctively want to gather a little of that fresh new growth and celebrate this most hopeful time of year by bringing it home with us. Natural decorations using flowers, leaves, twigs, feathers and moss give a fresh feel to spring-cleaned rooms, when doors and windows can once more be thrown open to let in the sweet spring air.

Dogwood heart

*I*n early spring, the young shoots of dogwood are particularly prominent before the shrub produces its foliage, and a few can easily be pruned without affecting the overall shape of the shrub. Use the shoots soon after cutting, while still pliable and full of sap, to make this charming wall decoration.

MATERIALS
~
generous bundle of dogwood shoots
florist's wire
secateurs (pruners)
natural raffia

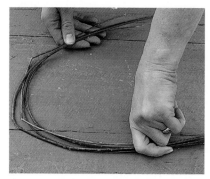

1 Select ten long shoots, and divide them into two bundles of five. Very carefully, bend each bundle into a large U-shape, easing the shoots as you go to avoid snapping them.

2 Hold the two U-shapes at right angles to each other to create a heart shape. Using the florist's wire, join the shapes where they cross. You will need to ease the dogwood into position very gently.

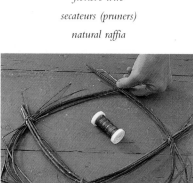

3 Wire the bottom point of the heart. Once you have established the shape, you may want to re-wire all the joints to hold them firmly in place. Trim any very long ends.

4 Build on the basic shape, thickening it up by adding some finer and shorter shoots to the top and securing them with wire.

5 Finish by binding all the joints with raffia. Make sure you cover all the wire. Finally, trim all the ends to neaten the heart and give it a pretty finished shape.

Spring napkin decoration

The sophisticated gold and white colour combination used in these elegant and exquisitely scented napkin decorations would be perfect for a formal dinner over the Easter holiday. The tiny bells of lily-of-the-valley harmonize visually with the pure white of the cyclamen.

MATERIALS
~

For each napkin:
sprig of small-leaved ivy
scissors
4-5 stems lily-of-the-valley
3 stems dwarf cyclamen
3 cyclamen leaves
gold cord

1 Fold the napkin into a rectangle, then roll it into a cylindrical shape. Wrap an ivy sprig around the middle of the napkin. Tie the stem firmly in a knot.

2 Take the lily-of-the-valley and cyclamen flowers and create a small sheaf in your hand by spiralling the stems. Place one cyclamen leaf at the back of the flowers for support, and two more around the cyclamen flowers to emphasize the focal point. Tie the stems with gold cord. Lay the flat back of the sheaf on top of the napkin and ivy, and wrap the excess gold cord around the napkin, gently tying it into a bow on top of the stems.

Left: Large, leathery leaves such as this Fatsia japonica, can be quickly fixed around napkins to make elegant, natural napkin rings.

Feather pictures

The feathers of domesticated fowl are a witty image for Eastertime, and simply mounted in picture frames they make original and effective decorations. The most successful compositions show a sympathy between frame and feathers, with a harmony of colours and proportions. A variety of feathers are readily available from fish-tackle suppliers, who sell them for fly-tying, but look out for them, too, on countryside walks.

Above: A piece of string appears to tie the bantam feather down, while the colour of the quill is echoed in the inner edge of the frame.

Above: Gloriously fluffy and softly hued, a female mallard's feather looks delightful filling a simple beechwood frame. Leaving the glass off the frame will add an extra dimension to the picture.

Left: Neatly tailored male pheasant feathers look wonderful in ordered lines. Two large feathers with a matching pair of small ones on either side make a more interesting composition. The soft grey of the frame, recycled from an old barn door, picks out the downy part of the feathers.

Willow and feather star

The neutral tones of willow and wild bird feathers harmonize beautifully and are easily transformed into wreaths and hangings. Light and airy in appearance, this delicate-looking star is surprisingly robust.

MATERIALS
~
secateurs (pruners)
18 willow boughs, about 40cm/16in long
natural raffia
scissors
high-tack craft glue
about 40 female pheasant feathers

1 Using secateurs (pruners), trim the boughs roughly to length. Lay three bundles, each of three sticks, on a flat surface to form a triangle. Use raffia to bind the corners.

2 Make a second triangle, using the rest of the boughs. Lay one triangle on top of the other to form a star and, using the raffia, bind together at the points where the triangles cross. Trim the ends of the boughs to neaten the shape.

3 Using the high-tack glue, stick the feathers to the inner hexagon of the star, wedging them between the sticks. To finish the points of the stars, tie pairs of feathers into V-shapes using raffia and glue them in position.

Nest table decoration

*I*n early spring, when there are still few flowers available for cutting, a nest makes a most delightful seasonal display. Quails' eggs lend a convincingly wild look to this display, but the eggs of other domesticated fowl, such as hens, ducks or geese, could also be used.

MATERIALS

~

8 willow boughs 15cm/6in long

secateurs (pruners)

15cm/6in diameter willow wreath

natural raffia

scissors

bin liner (trash bag)

sphagnum moss

small feathers

5 quails' eggs

1 The willow boughs make up the base of the nest, so trim them to fit across the wreath.

2 Use short lengths of raffia to tie the willow boughs to the base of the wreath.

3 Turn the nest right side up. Cut a circle of plastic sheet from the bin liner (trash bag) to line the nest, making it large enough to cover the bottom and reach a little way up the sides. Tease out enough moss to line the nest.

4 Arrange the moss loosely for a natural look. Add a few feathers, carefully lay the quails' eggs in the nest, and finish with a few more feathers.

Decorated Eggs

~

ince ancient times the egg has been seen as a potent good luck token, a gift bringing with it the promise of good health and fortune, and the exchange of eggs at Easter is an old and highly symbolic tradition. Many styles of dyeing and decoration have evolved, using various resist techniques, scratched designs, hand-painting and gilding. If you want to serve coloured eggs for breakfast on Easter morning, use either a natural vegetable dye or edible food colouring. Fabric dyes offer a wider range of colours for eggs that are not going to be eaten.

Easter display

*C*oloured eggs will immediately transform spring flowers into an Easter display. Simplicity is the secret: just gather together an abundance of flowers and add a few eggs, carefully laid on moss to evoke the idea of a nest.

MATERIALS
~

hard-boiled eggs

paper towels

food colouring (if eggs are to be eaten)

or cold-water fabric dye

glass jar for each dye

vinegar

salt

tulips or other spring flowers

scissors

vase

moss

plate

3 When the egg has reached the desired colour, lift it out and repeat with the rest. The dye solution will become weaker as you dye more eggs, so each will need to be left longer to achieve the same shade. Cut 1cm/½in off the end of each flower stem and arrange in a vase. Arrange the coloured eggs on a nest of moss on a plate.

1 Rinse the hard-boiled eggs in cold water and pat them dry on paper towels. To mix the dye, pour half a small bottle of food colouring or put half a disc of fabric dye into a glass jar, then pour on 300ml/½ pint/1¼ cups hot water.

2 Add 30ml/2 tbsp vinegar and 15ml/ 1 tbsp salt. Lower an egg into the jar of dye and leave for a few minutes. Check the colour regularly.

Above: Simple displays of spring flowers can be grouped together to increase their impact. Make the most of their pure beauty by massing one type only in each container.

Bleached spiral eggs

Highly intricate designs can be created on eggshells using this traditional decorating technique. To start with, try a simple spiral motif in an all-over design. Use only the tiniest amount of bleach and work in a well-ventilated area. If you are not wearing rubber gloves, do not let the bleach touch your skin. Natural wood dyes are available from craft shops.

MATERIALS
~

egg drill or darning needle

pump

white eggs

bowl

natural dye: logwood or walnut shell

stainless steel saucepan

slotted spoon

bleach

egg cup

fine paintbrush

paper towels

1 First blow the eggs. Pierce the narrow end of each egg with the drill, insert the pump and gently pump out the contents. Alternatively, make a small hole in each end of the egg using a needle and blow out the contents. Wash out the shell.

2 Put 30ml/2 tbsp of each dye in a saucepan three-quarters full of water and bring to the boil. Add the eggs to the pan one at a time, making sure that the shell is fully covered. Leave the egg in the dye until it becomes very dark.

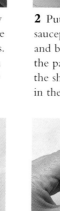

3 Pour a little bleach into an egg cup and paint the spirals on to the egg. Paint dots between the spirals. Leave for about 30 seconds to allow the bleach to eat away at the dyed surface.

4 Wipe away the bleach with a paper towel to reveal the white surface below the dye.

Natural dyed eggs

*V*egetable dyes are prepared by boiling an organic matter in water. The longer the water boils before the egg is added, the stronger the colour.

MATERIALS
~

hard-boiled eggs
candle, wax crayon or a piece of beeswax
natural dyes: turmeric, spinach, beetroot
(beets) or tea leaves
stainless steel saucepan for each dye
paper towels

1 Draw any kind of pattern you want on the hard-boiled eggs using a candle, wax crayon or piece of beeswax.

2 Make up batches of various dyes in separate saucepans, and boil the eggs for 5 minutes in the colours of your choice.

3 Lift out the eggs and pat them dry with paper towels to reveal the patterns.

Left: Display hard-boiled eggs in bright primary colours and arrange them in a cheerful straw nest strewn with tiny chocolate eggs, or wrap them in shimmering coloured net (tulle) tied with matching satin ribbons.

Onion skin eggs

Eggs can be boiled in a saucepan of onion skin dye and served for breakfast on Easter Day. Boil the onion skins first to release their colour before adding the eggs; the colour of the dye can be deepened by adding red onion skins to the water.

MATERIALS
~

large handful of onion skins

stainless steel saucepan

brown eggs

slotted spoon

metal scouring pad

1 Put the onion skins in a pan three-quarters full of water. Bring to the boil and simmer for 5–10 minutes to release the colour. Add the eggs to the saucepan, topping up the water to cover them, and allow to boil gently:
4 minutes for soft-boiled eggs;
10 minutes for hard-boiled eggs.

2 Remove the eggs from the pan with a slotted spoon. Cool hard-boiled eggs under cold running water and, while still wet, scratch the shells all over with a scouring pad for a mottled effect.

Blue and white eggs

*B*lue and white patterns always look fresh, and this is a chic and simple decoration. The design is created by sticking on small squares of masking tape, then stippling on the colour using a stencil brush. The largest egg of this group is big enough to include a witty motif, stencilled in place before arranging the checks around it.

MATERIALS

~

scissors

masking tape

hard-boiled white eggs

stencil brush

stencil paint

paper towels

1 Decide on the size of your checks and cut several strips of masking tape to the correct width.

2 Cut squares from the strips and begin sticking them to each egg in checker-board fashion. Start with a band three squares wide all around the length of the egg, leaving the narrow end free, then fill in as much of the rest of the shell as possible. At the wide end, you will need to adjust the squares to fit, even cutting triangles if appropriate.

3 Dip the tip of the stencil brush into the paint, dab off the excess on paper towels, then apply the paint using a gentle dabbing motion for a subtle stippled effect. Allow the paint to dry completely before carefully peeling off the masking tape.

Découpage eggs

*T*he art of paper-cutting has a long tradition in Switzerland, where it is used to make greetings cards and pictures. This technique can be combined with the Victorian art of découpage – decorating surfaces using cut-out motifs – to create decorated eggs that don't demand intricate paintbrush skills. Eggs that are to be eaten should not be decorated using this technique.

MATERIALS
~

sharp-pointed scissors

selection of coloured papers

tracing paper and pencil

paperclips

craft knife

cutting mat

pinking shears

blown white eggs

wallpaper paste

acrylic matt varnish

small varnish brush

1 Cut a piece of coloured paper to 20 x 15cm/8 x 6in and fold it in half. Trace the template, secure it to the folded paper with paperclips and cut it out carefully. Using pinking shears, cut two strips of a different-coloured paper, 3mm/⅛in wide and long enough to fit around the egg lengthways. Use scissors to cut a second strip the same length in the first colour.

2 Mix the wallpaper paste according to the manufacturer's instructions. Using your finger, smear the surface of each egg and the back of the motifs with the wallpaper paste, taking care not to let any of it get on to the front of the paper. Position a bird motif on both sides of each egg.

3 Smear a little wallpaper paste on the edging strips and position these around the eggs between the motifs. Trim the strips to length if necessary.

4 Allow the eggs to dry completely, leaving them overnight if possible. When dry, coat the eggs with acrylic matt varnish and leave to dry.

Leaf-stencilled eggs

Eggs and new leaves are both powerful symbols of spring, and here they have been combined in an exquisite decoration. The eggs are first dyed — some in a sharp leaf green, others in a softer, moss green — then stencilled using a combination of blue-greens and mossy greens. The overall effect is co-ordinated yet full of variety.

MATERIALS
~

cold-water fabric dye

glass jar or bowl

salt

blown white eggs

metal spoon

paper towels

all-purpose glue

small fern leaves

stencil brush

stencil paint

1 Mix the dye according to the manufacturer's instructions, and add the specified amount of salt. Lower an egg into the dye. Check the egg after a few minutes, and if it has reached the colour you want, take it out with a spoon and let it drain on paper towels.

2 When the egg is dry, wipe it all over with a paper towel. Place a thin film of glue on the back of a leaf and smooth the leaf on to the shell.

3 Dip the tip of the stencil brush into the stencil paint and dab off the excess on paper towels. The brush should be almost dry. Gently apply a thin film of paint using a stippling motion. This will give a speckled effect, allowing the undercoat to show through.

4 When the paint is dry to the touch (it will dry quickly), carefully peel off the leaf. Allow the paint to dry before arranging the eggs in a bowl.

Geometric gilding

These eggs are decorated with gold and silver gilt wax, which is polished to a shine. The eggs look stunning suspended from the branches of freshly gathered pussy willow.

MATERIALS
~
blown eggs
acrylic paint
flat paintbrush
white pencil
picture framer's wax gilt in gold and silver
soft cloth
wire egg holders

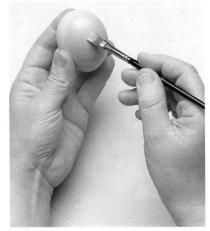

1 Paint each egg with acrylic paint: do this in two stages, allowing one side to dry before painting the other side.

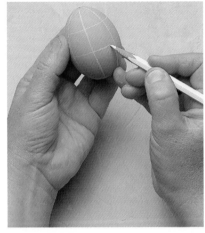

2 Using a white pencil, draw horizontal and vertical lines over the egg to make a large checkered pattern.

3 Paint on the gold wax gilt in alternate squares, taking care to keep the edges neat. Leave to dry for about 10 minutes, then paint on the silver squares and leave to dry.

4 Polish the eggs lightly with a soft cloth to a deep shine. Don't worry if some of the acrylic paint begins to show through as this adds to the effect.

5 Hold the two prongs of the wire holder firmly together and push them into the hole at the top of each egg.

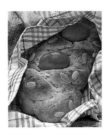

Easter Treats

~

As one of the major festivals of the Christian calendar, Easter has acquired a wealth of culinary traditions that can be drawn on for family feasts and parties. Easter dishes are rich in symbolism, from coloured boiled eggs eaten for breakfast on Easter Day to roast lamb with its distant echoes of ancient rites. Treat your family to a simnel cake or a slice of rich and creamy pashka. And no traditional Easter celebration would be complete without hot cross buns on Good Friday and masses of chocolate eggs.

Truffle-filled Easter egg

Moulding your own chocolate Easter egg is very rewarding and the egg makes a very special gift, especially when filled with luxurious home-made truffles. You will need two 15cm/6in plastic Easter egg moulds.

INGREDIENTS
~

350g/12oz plain (semisweet), milk or
white chocolate, melted
For the truffles:
250ml/8fl oz/1 cup double (heavy) cream
285g/10oz fine quality bittersweet or plain
(semisweet) chocolate, chopped
45g/1½oz/3 tbsp unsalted butter, cubed
45ml/1½fl oz/3 tbsp brandy
cocoa powder, for dusting

MELTING CHOCOLATE
Set a small heatproof bowl over a pan of barely simmering water. Without letting the water in the pan come to a boil, place the pieces of broken chocolate in the bowl. Lower the heat and allow the chocolate to melt gently, stirring frequently.

---

1 Make the truffles. Bring the cream to the boil over a medium heat, then remove the pan from the heat and add the chocolate pieces. Stir until the chocolate has melted. Stir in the butter until it melts and add the brandy. Strain into a bowl and cool. Cover and refrigerate overnight.

4 Unmould the egg halves. Insert a knife point between the chocolate and the mould to break the air lock. Hold the mould open side down and squeeze to release the half egg. Repeat with the other half and refrigerate.

2 Use a tablespoon or a melon baller to scrape the mixture into about 30 balls. Sift the cocoa on to a plate and roll the truffle balls in the cocoa, using the palm of your hand. Refrigerate the truffles until needed. (They should be used within one week.)

3 For the chocolate egg, line a baking (cookie) sheet with baking parchment. Spoon the melted chocolate into the chocolate egg moulds, pouring out any excess, then place the moulds open side down on the baking sheet. Refrigerate for 2 minutes. Apply a second coat of chocolate and refrigerate for 3 minutes more. Repeat a third time and chill for at least 1 hour or until set. Reserve any leftover chocolate.

5 Hold one egg half with a paper towel and fill with the truffles. Spread a little melted chocolate on to the rim and press on the other half, making sure the rims match up. Hold for 4 seconds, then refrigerate until completely set.

Simnel cake

*H*alfway through Lent it is *traditional to bake a simnel cake, to be brought out in celebration of Easter Day and the end of the lenten fast. This rich fruit cake contains a layer of marzipan in the centre and is topped with marzipan decorations.*

INGREDIENTS
~

butter, for greasing
500g/1¼lb marzipan
175g/6oz/1 cup icing (confectioners')
sugar, sifted, plus extra for dusting
225g/8oz/2 cups raisins
175g/6oz/1 cup sultanas (golden raisins)
50g/2oz/⅓ cup glacé (candied) cherries,
quartered
50g/2oz/⅓ cup chopped mixed candied
(citrus) peel
175g/6oz/¾ cup butter, softened
175g/6oz/¾ cup caster (superfine) sugar
4 eggs
225g/8oz/2 cups plain (all-purpose) flour
5ml/1 tsp baking powder
5ml/1 tsp ground mixed spice (allspice)
60ml/4 tbsp apricot jam
purple and green food colouring
ribbon, to decorate

1 Grease and double-line a cake tin (pan) and preheat the oven to 160°C/ 325°F/Gas 3. Reserving 50g/2oz marzipan for the decoration, cut the rest in half and roll out thinly on a surface lightly dusted with icing (confectioners') sugar. Using the base of an 18cm/7in round cake tin, cut out the marzipan round.

3 Place half the mixture in the cake tin and level the surface. Lay the marzipan round on top. Add the remaining cake mixture, smooth the top and make a slight depression in the centre. Bake for 2–2½ hours until golden brown. Cool in the tin then turn out on to a wire rack to cool completely. To make the apricot glaze, heat the jam gently in a saucepan, then strain into a bowl.

2 Combine the raisins, sultanas (golden raisins), glacé (candied) cherries and mixed candied (citrus) peel. In another bowl, cream the butter with the sugar until light and fluffy. Add three of the eggs, one at a time, beating well after each addition. Sift in the flour, baking powder and mixed spice (allspice) and fold in gently. Add the mixed fruit and fold in until evenly mixed.

4 Roll out two-thirds of the reserved marzipan and trim to an 18cm/7in circle. Brush the top of the cake with apricot glaze and cover with the marzipan round. From the trimmings of the marzipan, shape 11 small egg shapes and form the rest into a rope long enough to go round the top of the cake. Secure the rope and eggs in place with the apricot glaze.

5 Separate the remaining egg and brush the marzipan evenly with egg yolk. Prepare a hot grill (broiler) and sit the cake on a baking (cookie) sheet. Grill (broil) the marzipan quickly until tinged with golden brown. Leave to cool.

6 Beat the egg white and icing (confectioners') sugar together until thick and glossy. Spread in the centre of the cake and leave to set. Colour the reserved marzipan and mould flowers to decorate the top of the cake. Finally, add the ribbon, tied with a pretty bow.

Hot cross buns

*F*ragrant spiced buns are delicious at any time of year, but these glossy fruit buns marked with pastry crosses are an essential ingredient in the traditional Easter celebration. Serve them warm with butter for breakfast or afternoon tea on Good Friday.

INGREDIENTS
~
250g/9oz/2½ cups strong white flour
250g/9oz/2½ cups wholemeal (whole-wheat) flour
5ml/1 tsp salt
10ml/2 tsp ground mixed spice (allspice)
50g/2oz/4 tbsp butter
15g/½oz dried yeast
50g/2oz/¼ cup soft brown sugar
275ml/9fl oz/1¼ cups warm milk
2 eggs, beaten
115g/4oz/1 cup currants
butter, for greasing
pastry, for crosses
For the glaze:
30ml/2 tbsp milk
25g/1oz/2 tbsp caster (superfine) sugar

1 Sift both flours, the salt and the mixed spice (allspice) into a bowl and rub in the butter. Activate the yeast with 5ml/ 1 tsp sugar and a little milk. Make a well in the flour and add the yeast mixture, the eggs and the rest of the milk. Mix to a dough. Add the currants. Cover and leave to rise for 2 hours.

2 Knock back the dough and knead briefly. Divide into 20–24 buns and place on a greased and floured baking (cookie) sheet. Cover and leave to rise until doubled in size. Preheat the oven to 190°C/375°F/Gas 5. Top each bun with a pastry cross, moistened with a little milk to stick to the dough. Bake in the oven for about 15–20 minutes.

3 To make the glaze, boil the milk and sugar to form a syrup and brush the cooked, hot buns with it. Leave to cool.

Festival shortbreads

This Mediterranean version of shortbread is baked for important religious festivals and keeps well for a long time, stored in a delicately flavoured sugar.

INGREDIENTS

~

250g/9oz/1 generous cup unsalted butter

65g/2½oz/⅓ cup caster (superfine) sugar

1 egg yolk

30ml/2 tbsp Greek ouzo, Pernod or brandy

115g/4oz unblanched almonds

65g/2½oz/1 generous cup cornflour (cornstarch)

300g/11oz/2½ cups plain (all-purpose) flour

60ml/4 tbsp triple-distilled rose water

500g/1¼lb/2¼ cups icing (confectioners') sugar, sifted

1 Preheat the oven to 180°C/350°F/Gas 4. In a mixing bowl, cream the butter and add the caster (superfine) sugar, egg yolk and alcohol.

2 Grind the almonds in their skins: they should be much coarser and browner than commercially ground almonds. Add to the butter mixture, then stir in the cornflour (cornstarch) and enough plain (all-purpose) flour to give a firm, soft dough.

3 Line two large baking (cookie) sheets with baking parchment. Divide the dough into 24–28 equal portions. Make them into little rolls, then bend them into crescents round your finger. Place on the baking sheets and bake for about 15 minutes. Check the shortbreads and reduce the oven temperature if they seem to be colouring. Bake for 5–10 minutes more. Remove the shortbreads from the oven and let cool.

4 Pour the rose water into a small bowl and put the sifted icing (confectioners') sugar into a larger one. Dip a shortbread into the rose water and sprinkle with icing sugar. Repeat until all the shortbreads are coated. Place the shortbreads in an airtight tin to store, packing them loosely to prevent them sticking together. Sift the remaining icing sugar over the shortbreads before securing the lid.

Easter bread

*A*ll over the world Easter celebrations involve elaborate preparations in the kitchen. This bread, complete with red-dyed eggs, is a part of the traditional Greek Easter feast.

INGREDIENTS
~

25g/1oz fresh yeast

120ml/4fl oz/½ cup warm milk

675g/1½lb/6 cups plain (all-purpose) flour

2 eggs, beaten

2.5ml/½ tsp caraway seeds

15ml/1 tbsp caster (superfine) sugar

15ml/1 tbsp brandy

50g/2oz/4 tbsp butter, melted

1 egg white, beaten

2–3 hard-boiled eggs, dyed with red food colouring

50g/2oz/⅓ cup split (halved) almonds

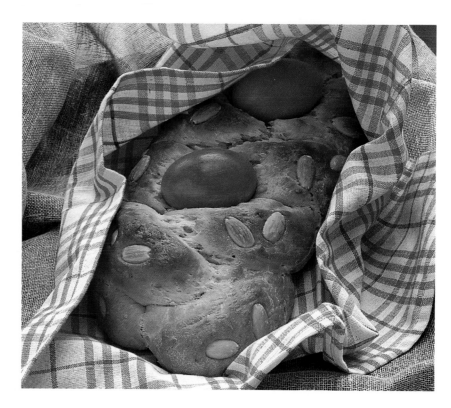

1 Crumble the yeast into a bowl and mix with a little warm water until softened. Add the milk and 115g/4oz/ 1 cup of the flour and mix to a creamy consistency. Cover with a cloth and leave in a warm place to rise for 1 hour.

2 Sift the remaining flour into a large bowl and make a well in the centre. Pour the risen yeast into the well and draw in a little flour from the sides. Add the eggs, caraway seeds, sugar and brandy. Incorporate the remaining flour to form a dough. Mix in the melted butter. Turn out on to a lightly floured surface and knead for about 10 minutes. Return to the bowl, cover with a cloth and leave in a warm place for 3 hours.

3 Preheat the oven to 180°C/350°F/ Gas 4. Knock back the dough, turn on to a lightly floured surface and knead for 1 minute. Divide the dough into three and roll each piece into a sausage. Make a plait (braid) and place on a greased baking (cookie) sheet. Tuck the ends under, brush with egg white and decorate with the coloured eggs and almonds. Bake for 1 hour, until the loaf sounds hollow when tapped on the bottom. Let cool.

Kulich

Special moulds are used to produce the characteristic shape of this Russian Easter cake, but clean terracotta flowerpots can be used instead. This quantity will fill two 15cm/6in pots.

INGREDIENTS
~

15ml/1 tbsp dried yeast

90ml/6 tbsp warm milk

75g/3oz/6 tbsp caster (superfine) sugar

500g/1¼lb/4 cups plain (all-purpose) flour

pinch saffron strands

30ml/2 tbsp dark rum

2.5ml/½ tsp ground cardamom

2.5ml/½ tsp ground cumin

50g/2oz/½ cup unsalted butter

2 eggs plus 2 egg yolks

1 vanilla pod, finely chopped

25g/1oz/2 tbsp chopped mixed candied (citrus) peel

25g/1oz/2 tbsp crystallized (candied) ginger

25g/1oz/2 tbsp chopped almonds

25g/1oz/2 tbsp currants

For the decoration:

75g/3oz/½ cup icing (confectioners') sugar

7.5–10ml/1½–2 tsp warm water

1 drop almond essence (extract)

crystallized violets, sugar roses and angelica

1 Combine the yeast, milk, 25g/1oz/2 tbsp sugar and 50g/2oz/½ cup flour until smooth. Leave in a warm place for 15 minutes until frothy. Soak the saffron in the rum for 15 minutes.

2 Sift the remaining flour and spices into a bowl and rub in the butter. Stir in the remaining sugar, make a well in the centre and work in the yeast mixture, the saffron liquid and the remaining ingredients to form a dough.

3 Knead the dough on a floured surface until smooth and elastic. Place in an oiled bowl, cover and leave in a warm place for 1 hour, until it has doubled in size.

4 Preheat the oven to 190°C/375°F/Gas 5. Grease, base-line and flour the flowerpot moulds. Knock back the dough, then divide it in half and form into rounds. Press the dough into the pots, cover and leave in a warm place for 30 minutes more, until the dough comes two-thirds of the way up the sides.

5 Bake in the preheated oven for about 50 minutes. Test the cakes with a skewer, then remove from the oven. Turn the cakes out on to a wire rack to cool.

6 Sift the icing (confectioners') sugar into a mixing bowl and blend with the water and almond essence (extract) to form a thick glacé icing. Pour the icing over the top of each cake, allowing it to drizzle down the sides, then scatter with crystallized violets, turquoise sugar roses and slivers of angelica.

Cowslip syllabub

*F*resh spring flowers add a
decorative touch to this simple
dessert, ideal to serve for Easter lunch.

CRYSTALLIZED FLOWERS

INGREDIENTS

~

200ml/7fl oz medium white wine
50g/2oz/4 tbsp caster (superfine) sugar
finely grated rind of 1 orange
juice of 1 orange
300ml/½ pint double (heavy) cream
32 cowslip flowers, fresh or crystallized
8 viola flowers, fresh or crystallized
fresh mint sprigs, to decorate
langue de chat biscuits, to serve

1 Place the wine, sugar, orange rind and orange juice in a bowl. Leave the mixture to stand for at least 2 hours.

2 Add the mixture to the cream a little at a time, whisking constantly until it stands in soft peaks. Spoon a little of the syllabub into the base of six serving glasses, and sprinkle a few of the cowslips and violas around the edges.

3 Continue to spoon the syllabub into the glasses to form a peak in the centre. Scatter with more of the flowers and chill in the fridge. Fix any remaining flowers to the *langue de chat* biscuits with a dab of icing, and serve the syllabub with the decorated biscuits.

1 For the crystallized flowers, first coat the petals or blooms with a thin, even layer of lightly beaten egg white. Use tweezers to dip the flowers into the egg white. The process must be done quickly before the egg white dries.

2 Sprinkle sifted icing (confectioners') sugar evenly over the flowers, shaking off any excess. Uneven patches of icing sugar will create an attractive light and dark shade contrast but the flowers will not be preserved as efficiently.

3 Place the coated flowers on a plate and allow them to dry. Stored between layers of tissue paper in a cool, dry place, the flowers should keep for about a week. Do not put sugar petals in the refrigerator or they will "weep".

Pashka

T his creamy Easter dessert is made in a special wooden mould but a terracotta flowerpot, well scrubbed and baked in a hot oven for 30 minutes, will do just as well. This version is scented with rose water and decorated with crystallized roses.

CRYSTALLIZED ROSES
Rinse and dry freshly picked full blooms. Coat each bloom with an even layer of lightly beaten egg white and sprinkle with icing (confectioners') sugar, shaking off any excess. Let dry on a wire rack before storing in an airtight container between layers of tissue paper. The roses will keep for about a week.

INGREDIENTS
~

60ml/4 tbsp single (light) cream
2 egg yolks
75g/3oz/⅓ cup caster (superfine) sugar
90g/3½oz/scant ½ cup unsalted butter
350g/12oz/1½ cups curd or ricotta cheese
350g/12oz/1½ cups mascarpone cheese
10ml/2 tsp triple-distilled rose water
50g/2oz/⅓ cup chopped candied (citrus) peel
50g/2oz/⅓ cup chopped blanched almonds
crystallized roses, to decorate

3 Line the flowerpot with muslin and spoon the mixture into it, covering the top with muslin. Weight a small plate on the top of the flowerpot and stand it on a plate in the fridge for about 6 hours, or overnight.

1 Heat the single (light) cream in a saucepan to just below boiling point. Beat the egg yolks in a mixing bowl with the caster (superfine) sugar until light and foamy, then add to the cream in the saucepan. Heat together until the mixture thickens, taking care not to let it boil and curdle. Remove the saucepan from the heat and set aside to cool.

2 Beat the butter until creamy and add to the cooled egg and cream mixture. Add the cheeses a little at a time, then add the rose water, candied (citrus) peel and chopped almonds.

4 Turn out the pashka by inverting the flowerpot on to a serving dish, and remove the muslin. Decorate the edge of the dish with crystallized roses.

Index